I Live in Two Homes

Adjusting to Divorce
and Remarriage

KIDS HAVE *TROUBLES* TOO

I Live in Two Homes

Adjusting to Divorce
and Remarriage

by Sheila Stewart and Rae Simons

Mason Crest Publishers

MASON CREST PUBLISHERS INC.
370 Reed Road
Broomall, Pennsylvania 19008
(866)MCP-BOOK (toll free)
www.masoncrest.com

First Printing
9 8 7 6 5 4 3 2 1

Library of Congress Cataloging-in-Publication Data

Stewart, Sheila, 1975–
 I live in two homes : adjusting to divorce and remarriage / by Sheila Stewart and Rae Simons.
     p. cm.
 Includes bibliographical references and index.
 ISBN (set) 978-1-4222-1691-0   ISBN 978-1-4222-1694-1
 ISBN (ppbk set) 978-1-4222-1904-1   ISBN (ppbk) 978-1-4222-1907-2
 1. Children of divorced parents—Juvenile literature. 2. Divorce—Juvenile literature. 3. Remarriage—Juvenile literature. I. Simons, Rae, 1957- II. Title.
 HQ777.5.S743 2010
 306.874—dc22
                                9517   2010012757
Design by MK Bassett-Harvey.
Produced by Harding House Publishing Service, Inc.
www.hardinghousepages.com
Cover design by Torque Advertising + Design.
Printed in USA by Bang Printing.

The creators of this book have made every effort to provide accurate information, but it should not be used as a substitute for the help and services of trained professionals.

Introduction

Each child is unique—and each child encounters a unique set of circumstances in life. Some of these circumstances are more challenging than others, and how a child copes with those challenges will depend in large part on the other resources in her life.

The issues children encounter cover a wide range. Some of these are common to almost all children, including threats to self-esteem, anger management, and learning to identify emotions. Others are more unique to individual families, but problems such as parental unemployment, a death in the family, or divorce and remarriage are common but traumatic events in many children's lives. Still others—like domestic abuse, alcoholism, and the incarceration of a family member—are unfortunately not uncommon in today's world.

Whatever problems a child encounters in life, understanding that he is not alone is a key component to helping him cope. These books, both their fiction and nonfiction elements, allow children to see that other children are in the same situations. The books make excellent tools for triggering conversation in a nonthreatening way. They will also promote understanding and compassion in children who may not be experiencing these issues themselves.

These books offer children important factual information—but perhaps more important, they offer hope.

—*Cindy Croft, M.A., Ed., Director of the Center for Inclusive Child Care*

"Are you ready, Celeste?" Mommy called up the stairs. "We have to leave!"

"Just a second!" Celeste yelled. She picked up Katie, her doll, and took one last look around the room to make sure she hadn't forgotten anything. She loved her room. She and Mommy had decorated it together and she thought it was the most beautiful room in the world. It had a brown and purple silky bedspread and matching curtains, with a fluffy purple rug on the floor.

Celeste turned off the light and went downstairs. Mommy was waiting by the backdoor, and Whitney, Celeste's little sister, was running around in the backyard.

"We have to go," Mommy said. "Daddy is expecting you at five."

Mostly, Celeste and Whitney lived with Mommy, but on some weekends and for a few weeks in the summer, they lived with Daddy. Mommy and Daddy had gotten divorced two years ago, when Celeste was only five, and Whitney was only three. Celeste still wished her parents could be together. She loved Mommy and she loved Daddy too, and she just wanted everybody to be together. She remembered when Mommy and Daddy had still lived together they had fought a lot, and they were mad all the time, but she thought they should be able to stop fighting and be friends again. After all, she fought with Whitney a lot but then they forgot about it and played together just fine.

Celeste started to get into the car but then stopped. "Wait!" she said to Mommy. "I think I forgot my sweater."

"Nope," Mommy said. "I put it in your suitcase. Get in the car."

"The purple sweater with the yellow butterflies on it?"

"That's the one."

Celeste got in the car and buckled up her seatbelt while Mommy got Whitney into the car and helped her with her seatbelt.

Daddy's house was in another town, and it took almost two hours to drive there. Celeste sometimes got tired of riding in the car, but she liked getting to see Daddy. Mommy played music on the radio, and Celeste read a book. Whitney looked at some books for a little while, too, but then she fell asleep.

By the time they got to Daddy's house it was starting to get dark. Earlier in the fall it had still been light when they got to Daddy's house. Then, sometimes, he let them play outside for a while before they had supper.

Whitney woke up when the car stopped and rubbed at her eyes.

"We're here!" Celeste told her.

Daddy came out of the house while Celeste and Whitney were getting out of the car.

"Celeste!" he said, swooping her up in a hug. She hugged him back. She liked the smell of him. Sometimes, at Mommy's house, she thought about that smell and felt sad.

Daddy put Celeste down and picked up Whitney. She was still sleepy, but Daddy tossed her into the air until she giggled.

Mommy got their suitcases out of the trunk and set them on the side of the driveway. Then she came over to give Celeste and Whitney hugs. Celeste didn't like this part. It was confusing how she could feel so happy about seeing Daddy at the

same time she was feeling sad about saying good-bye to Mommy.

"I love you, Celeste," Mommy said, hugging her. "I'll see you in a couple of days."

"I love you too, Mommy." Celeste held onto her mother for an extra-long minute.

After Mommy left, Celeste and Whitney went in the house with Daddy.

"I'm making some cheeseburgers," Daddy said. "Why don't you take your suitcases to your rooms and then come help me set the table?"

Celeste grabbed her suitcase and ran down the hall to her room. Her room at Daddy's house didn't have quite as much stuff in it as her room at Mommy's house, but she liked this room too. She had a pink and purple bedspread here and a big poster of ballerinas.

She put Katie on the bed and set the suitcase down beside the wall. She kept some clothes at Daddy's house, but she always brought stuff with her too. She decided not to unpack the suitcase and instead walked back down the hall to see Daddy again.

Later, at supper, Daddy put down his cheeseburger and looked at Celeste and Whitney.

"Tomorrow, I have a surprise for you," he said.

"Are we going to the zoo?" Whitney asked, but Daddy shook his head.

"There's somebody I want you to meet," he said, and then he wouldn't say any more about it.

After Celeste went to bed that night, she thought about the mysterious person Daddy wanted them to meet. Why would he want them to meet someone? Maybe it was somebody famous. Or somebody exciting, like a circus performer or a helicopter pilot.

She fell asleep wondering about it.

"Are we going to meet the person now?" Celeste asked at breakfast.

"At lunch," Daddy said. "And then I thought maybe we could all go to the science museum."

"Yay!" Whitney shouted.

Celeste was happy about the science museum too, but she still couldn't stop wondering about the person they were going to meet.

They went to lunch at a little restaurant across the street from the museum. As soon as they walked in, Celeste started looking around, trying to figure out who the person might be. She saw one man sitting by himself, but she hoped he wasn't the person, because he looked very grumpy.

"There she is," Daddy said, and started walking across the restaurant.

Celeste and Whitney followed him, but when Celeste saw where he was heading, she was confused. The table he was walking toward had two people sitting at it, not one. One of the people was a girl who looked like she was a little older than Celeste, and the other person was a woman about

Daddy's age. The girl had blonde hair that was tied up in a ponytail and she was wearing a blue turtleneck.

When he got to the table, Daddy leaned down and kissed the woman on the cheek. Whitney stopped walking suddenly, and Celeste ran into her.

"Why did Daddy kiss that lady?" Whitney whispered to Celeste.

Celeste shrugged. She had a strange feeling about this.

"Girls," Daddy said, waving them closer to the table, "this is Marcy. She's a friend of mine. And this is her daughter Jordan. She's nine; right, Jordan?"

The girl nodded, but she didn't say anything. She was staring at Celeste and Whitney, looking at one of them and then back to the other.

Slowly, Celeste pulled out a chair and sat down across from the woman. Whitney sat down next to her, and Daddy sat on the end, between Celeste and the woman.

"Hi Celeste, hi Whitney," the woman—Marcy— said. "I've heard so much about you."

"We haven't heard anything about you," Whitney said, and Celeste kicked her under the table.

Marcy laughed though. "That's okay," she said. "I'm sure we're going to be friends. And I'm sure you girls and Jordan will all get along wonderfully."

Celeste looked at Jordan. She wasn't sure about that at all. Jordan had stopped staring at them and was staring down at the table instead. She didn't look happy. Or friendly.

During lunch, Daddy and Marcy did most of the talking. Celeste and Whitney and Jordan answered questions when Daddy or Marcy asked them things, but mostly they just nibbled at their food.

After lunch, they all walked across the road to the science museum. Celeste noticed that Daddy was holding hands with Marcy. Whitney, though, decided to start talking to Jordan. She walked along beside her, asking questions—What grade was she in at school? Did she have any brothers or sisters? What was her favorite color?

Jordan answered some of Whitney's questions and sometimes she just shrugged her shoulders and didn't say anything. Celeste started feeling sorry for her. Whitney could be a pain sometimes.

"You can just ignore her if she's bugging you," Celeste told Jordan. "She's annoying sometimes."

"Hey!" Whitney said. "That's mean!"

Jordan glanced at Celeste. "Yes," she said. "I think little sisters would be annoying."

There was something about the way she said it that made Celeste feel strange again. She didn't know why, but she felt like something was going on that she didn't quite understand.

The science museum was fun, but only when Celeste avoided Jordan. Once or twice, she and Jordan accidentally started laughing together, when they ended up standing together next to each other and playing with the same activity. When Jordan noticed what she was doing though, she stopped laughing and walked away.

On Sunday evening, Daddy drove Celeste and Whitney back to Mommy's house.

"What did you think of Marcy?" he asked them.

"She's nice," Whitney said. Whitney thought everybody was nice unless they were actually mean to her.

"She was fine," said Celeste. She hadn't really paid much attention to Marcy, though. The only thing that was really interesting about her was that Daddy had kissed her and held her hand. Celeste wanted Daddy to kiss Mommy again and hold Mommy's hand.

After Daddy had left them with Mommy, Whitney started telling her all about the weekend.

"There was this lady named Marcy," Whitney said, "and Daddy kissed her."

Celeste looked at Mommy to see what she would say, but all Mommy did was raise her eyebrows and say, "Oh, really?" Celeste couldn't tell what she was thinking.

When Mommy was tucking her in that night, Celeste asked her, "Are you mad about Daddy kissing that woman?"

"No," Mommy said. "I'm not."

"Are you sad?" Celeste asked.

"No," Mommy said. "Are you upset about it?"

"No," Celeste said quickly, and then added, "I don't know. It makes me feel weird."

"He's always going to be your Daddy," Mommy said. "Just like I'm always going to be your Mommy. We both love you very much."

"I wish you could be married to each other again," Celeste said.

"I know," Mommy said, "but that's not going to happen."

"I know," Celeste said, "but I wish it could."

For the next couple of months, every time Celeste and Whitney went to Daddy's house, Marcy and Jordan were there. Or, at least, they spent some time there every weekend.

One Saturday in February, Daddy told Celeste and Whitney he wanted to talk to them. Marcy and Jordan had been over earlier in the day, but they had to leave so Jordan could go to a birthday party.

"Sit down," Daddy said. "We need to talk about something."

Celeste sat down on the couch feeling nervous. Daddy looked very serious.

"You both know how I feel about Marcy, right?" Daddy asked.

"She's your friend," Whitney said.

Celeste just stared at him.

"I love her," Daddy said. "I've asked her to marry me and she's said yes."

"Oh." Celeste couldn't think of anything else to say.

"Can I be in the wedding?" Whitney asked.

"Of course," Daddy said. "You both can."

Daddy and Marcy were going to get married in May. Celeste soon discovered that this marriage was going to mean more changes in her life that she didn't like. Marcy and Jordan were going to move into Daddy's house after the wedding and, because there were only three bedrooms, Celeste and Whitney were going to have to share a room.

"But I don't want to share a room with her," Celeste complained to Daddy.

"I'm sorry," Daddy said, "but Marcy and I can't afford to buy a bigger house right now."

"But why can't Whitney share a room with Jordan?" she asked.

"Jordan has to move to a new house," Daddy said. "She has a lot more changes happening in her life than you do."

Celeste glared at him and stomped back to her room—it was still going to be her room for another few weeks. She slammed the door and threw herself on her bed. She'd thought it was bad before, with Mommy and Daddy living in different houses, but this was worse. She missed the old days, when Daddy spent the weekends playing with her and Whitney. Now it seemed like Marcy and Jordan were always around. Celeste missed Daddy being just theirs.

On the weekend before the wedding, Daddy said they had to move all Whitney's stuff into Celeste's room, and he wanted to Celeste to make space for it.

Celeste went in her room and looked at it. This was the last time it was going to be just hers. She'd found some wide black tape in a drawer in the kitchen and now she put a strip of tape down the middle of the floor. She made a little path to the door with the tape, so that Whitney would be able to get in and out without walking on Celeste's side of the room. Then she pushed all of her things from Whitney's side to her side. They made a messy pile.

She went out and told Daddy she was done. He came in and looked at the room. She wanted him to be mad about the tape on the floor and the mess, but instead he just said, "Looks good. Thanks, Celeste."

On the day before the wedding, Daddy's parents picked Celeste and Whitney up from Mommy's house and took them to a church near Daddy's house. They were having a rehearsal for the wedding. Celeste, Whitney, and Jordan were all going to be junior bridesmaids, even though Celeste overheard Grandma say they were too young.

The rehearsal was mostly boring. Celeste and the other girls practiced walking up the aisle a few times and then sat down while Daddy and Marcy practiced doing their part.

"I hate this," Jordan said, kicking the seat in front of her.

"Me too," Celeste said. "Nothing's been the same since Daddy started dating your mom."

Jordan looked at her. "You think it's been better for me? Mom and I had lots of fun before your dad came around. We were fine without you guys."

They were quiet for a little bit. "I'm sorry," Celeste said finally. "It's not your fault."

"Yeah," Jordan said. "It's not yours either. And your dad's pretty cool, I guess."

"So we can all be friends now?" Whitney asked, and Celeste laughed. She and Jordan looked at each other again.

"I guess so," Jordan said.

"It could be nice to have a big sister," Celeste said.

"I've never had any brothers or sisters at all," Jordan said. "Just don't borrow my clothes without asking and we'll be fine."

They all laughed together. Celeste felt better than she had in a long time. Things would never be the same as they had been, she knew, but that didn't mean they couldn't be good. Things were always changing in life and this change, she thought, was actually pretty good.

Kids and Divorce

Most kids have friends whose parents are divorced. Maybe your parents are divorced. Maybe you have a stepmom or a stepdad—or both. All those things mean big changes in your life.

And changes can be scary. It's only normal to feel that way.

What Is a Divorce?

A divorce is what happens after a husband and wife decide they no longer want to be married to each other. It means they will no longer live together. They will sign legal papers that make them no longer married. Now they will both be single again. Their marriage is over. They can marry other people if they want to.

Once a husband and wife are divorced, they probably won't ever go back to being married again. Being divorced is a big decision. If your mom and dad are divorced, they thought about it a lot before they decided to stop being married. It's not something they did lightly, on the spur of the moment, just because they happened to be mad at each other one day. They probably spent a long time trying to fix the problems in the marriage before they decided to get divorced. When they couldn't fix the problems, they decided that divorce was the best solution for everyone.

Divorce Is Hard

But divorce is never easy, even for the grownups involved. Going through a divorce often makes people sad and upset. Sometimes both the husband and wife want a divorce, but sometimes one wants to and the other one doesn't. When that happens, it's hard for both sides. Even if both sides agree that divorce is the best solution, both of them will probably feel sad and disappointed that their marriage didn't last.

Divorce is hard for the kids in the family too. Kids don't like to hear their parents fighting all the time—but they also like to have both parents there. Change is hard for kids. It's hard to get used to all the changes that divorce brings. So kids usually feel sad and upset too. By the time parents tell their kids they're getting divorced, the grownups have probably had a while to get used to the idea, but it may come as an unpleasant surprise to the kids. They may feel angry, sad, confused, and scared.

Divorces Isn't a Kid's Fault!

When parents get divorced, their marriage ends—but they NEVER divorce their kids. A divorce doesn't change the fact that your dad is your dad, and your mom is your mom. The problems in their marriage are between the two of them. They're not your fault, and they both still love you as much as ever. Even if you don't all live together any more—and that's really sad—you still belong to both your mom and your dad.

When a marriage isn't working anymore, everyone in the family is affected. Though it is hard to deal with, sometimes divorce is the best option.

Sometimes kids feel as though they're the ones who made the divorce happen. This isn't true. If your parents are divorced, it didn't happen because you got in trouble at school or got bad grades or didn't keep your room clean. Even if your mom and dad fought ABOUT you sometimes, that's still not your fault! Divorce is caused by grownup problems.

Marital Status, 2009

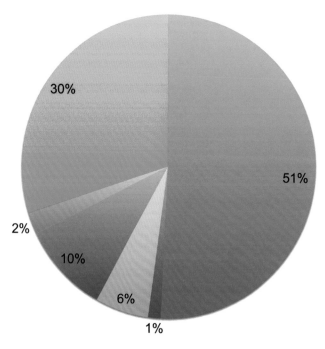

30%

51%

2%

10%

6%

1%

- Married Spouse Present - Married Spouse Absent - Widowed
- Divorced - Separated - Never Married

Divorce is very common in the United States. According to a 2009 survey from the U.S. Census Bureau, 10% of people questioned were divorced. However, there are statistics showing that since 2008, almost half of all marriages have ended in divorce.

Kids Can't Make the Divorce Go Away

If your parents are divorced, you didn't make it happen—and you can't fix it either. That's not your job. Maybe you've seen movies where kids plotted and planned, and eventually managed to get their divorced parents back together. It makes a nice story—but it doesn't usually happen that way. Lots of kids wish it could be true. They wish things could go back to "normal," the way things used to be when they were younger. But that's probably not going to happen. And again, that's not their fault!

Learning to Cope with Divorce

Sometimes it's hard to accept that you can't do anything to change a situation. You feel as though there has to be SOMETHING you can do to make life go back to being the way you want it to be. Part of growing up, though, is learning that there are some situations in life—and parents' divorce is one of them—that we can't change. We just have to accept them. We have to learn to deal with them as **positively** as we can. We can't change the situation, but we CAN change our attitude about it.

When kids feel upset about their parents' divorce, they often don't know how to handle their feelings. Maybe they know they're SUPPOSED to act like they're happy, like they're **mature** kids who please their parents—but at the same time, they feel angry their life has changed and no one gave them any choice in the matter! They feel scared because they don't know for sure what will happen next. They feel sad and lonely because they miss the parent that no longer lives with them all the time.

All those angry, scared, sad feelings have to come out somewhere. If you don't talk about them, they may come out in the wrong ways. You may find that you're getting in trouble more often—or that you're not doing as well on your homework—or that you're getting in more fights with your brother or sister—or that you find yourself being rude to your mom or dad or your teacher.

Understand the Word

If you handle something **positively**, you decide to treat it as though it were a good thing rather than a bad thing. You make up your mind to act as happy as you can about it.

Someone who is **mature** acts in a grownup way.

It's perfectly normal to feel upset after a divorce. Your parents will understand that, and so will your teachers at school. But everyone will be happier—including you!—if you can find ways to express your feelings that don't hurt other people. Talk to your parents about your feelings and ask for their help. They may have ideas that will help you deal with your feelings better.

Try drawing pictures when you feel upset and let all your upset feelings come out in the picture. Or listen to music. Go outside and run around until you're tired. Dance. Play an instrument. Write a story. Get your feelings out **creatively**.

Ask your librarian to help you find books about divorce that are written for kids your age. Books like that can help you understand what's happening. And they can help you feel as though you're not so all alone.

But the most important thing is to talk to someone. If you can't talk to your parents, talk to your friends about your feelings. Talk to

Understand the Word

If you do something **creatively**, you find ways to express your feelings as you do it. You bring something new to the world—whether it's a drawing, a poem, a song, or a new idea—when you act creatively, so it not only helps you but it also makes the world a richer place.

your teacher. Talk to your brothers and sisters (after all, they're going through the same thing you are.) Maybe you can talk to a grandparent or an aunt or uncle.

When you're very upset, it can sometimes be hard to concentrate. You may have a hard time paying attention in school or focusing on your homework. You may not feel like eating. You may have more bad dreams than normal. When those things happen, you may need some extra help. Let your parents and teacher know if that's happening. If you think you need more help, ask if you can talk to your school **counselor**. Let a grownup you trust know that you need help dealing with your feelings.

And if you have a friend whose parents are going through a divorce, be a good listener. Let your friend know you want to hear about his or her feelings.

Knowing that other people understand our feelings helps us be able to cope with them better.

Understand the Word

A **counselor** is a person who has been specially trained to talk with people in order to help them deal with their feelings. Counselors work in schools, but they also may have their own offices.

What Happens Next?

If your parents get divorced, you may feel like your whole life has fallen apart. You may think it will never get put back together. But gradually, as time goes by, you will start to notice that you're building a new world. Things that once felt strange will now feel normal. That's the just the way life works. Sooner or later, we get used to things, even things we don't like.

Divorce can make you feel mad, sad, and confused and you might have a hard time talking to your parents about your feelings. Speaking to a psychologist or a school counselor can help you sort out all these feelings.

When parents get divorced, usually one of them moves out of the house and lives somewhere else. Some kids spend about half of their time living with one parent and the other half living with the other. Most kids live most of the time with one parent and visit the other. How often you visit your other parent will probably depend on where he or she lives. No matter how often you go back and forth, whether it's every weekend or once a month, you will probably feel strange at first having two homes—but again, this is something you will get used to.

Sometimes divorced parents can have a hard time working out all the details. Who gets the kids for holidays? Who has them on their birthdays? These can be hard questions to work out. Another problem may be deciding on the kids' rules. If your parents are divorced, maybe your mom insists you go to bed by 8:00 every night—but your dad lets you stay up till whenever you get sleepy. Maybe your dad won't let you eat soda and junk food—but your mom will. Different rules can be confusing for the kids involved—and they can make the grownups involved feel upset too.

Sometimes divorced parents still have angry feelings toward each other—and the kids can get caught up in fights. When that happens, it's a bad situation for the kids. Nobody likes to be caught in the middle during a fight between two people. If you ever feel like that's happening to you, talk to your parents and let them know how you're feeling. Ask them to solve their problems without involving you.

Eventually one or both of your parents may decide to get married again. When that happens, you'll have to deal with a whole new set of changes. You may feel as though you just got used to the "new normal"—and now the grownups are changing everything all over again!

Step-Families

If your mom or dad get married again, suddenly you'll have a new adult in your life. You may have a lot of questions. Like—

What are you supposed to call him or her?
Does this new person have the right to set the rules
 for you?

Can she yell at you? Can he punish you if you get in trouble?

Do you have to obey her?

What if he doesn't like you? What if she's mean to you?

Is he or she going to try to take your REAL mom's or dad's place?

These are all normal questions to have. Talk about them with your parents. Some of the answers will be up to you and some won't.

For instance, you can probably decide what you want to call a stepparent. You might want use his or her first name. Or if you call your mother "Mom," you might decide to call your stepmother "Mother." You might start out with one answer to this question, and then after a while, decide that some other word or name seems more natural.

But yes, you do need to listen to your stepparents. A stepparent is another adult who's looking out for you, the way a teacher at school does or a coach. So whether or not you feel close to a stepparent, you need to give him or her that same kind of respect.

Fairy tales have given stepparents, especially stepmothers, a bad reputation. It's always the wicked stepmother who tries to hurt Snow White or makes Cinderella do all the dirty work. But those are just stories. Remember—your dad or mom loves this person, so chances are, he or she must be pretty nice. Stepparents can feel uncertain and shy too. It's a new situation

Fairy tales like Snow White and Cinderella make stepmothers into evil characters. The truth is that a stepparent is just another adult who is there to care for you. Give your new stepparent a chance and you are likely to have a good relationship with him or her.

for them too, and they may worry they'll do or say the wrong thing. Give yourselves a chance to get used to each other, and things will eventually seem more natural. Hopefully, you'll end up with a new person in your life who loves you and whom you love in return.

Understand the Word

A **compromise** is when each side in an argument gives up something they want and each side gets something they want.

And you don't ever need to worry about your stepparent taking your mom's or dad's place. Your heart has a big space inside it. There's room in it for lots of people and lots of different kinds of relationships. But your mom will always be your mom, and your dad will always be your dad. No one and nothing will ever change that!

What if You Can't Get Along?

Any time people share a home, they will be faced with lots of conflicts. Being in a family—whether it's your birth family or a stepfamily—means you have to learn to **compromise**. Sometimes, it's also okay to speak up and let people know if you don't think something is fair, so long as you do it respectfully, without yelling and crying and pouting.

If you REALLY can't seem to get along with your stepparent no matter what you try, though, it's okay to ask for help. Talk to your parents. Talk to your stepparent—but remember that your stepparent has feelings. If you shout at him or her, "I can't stand you! I wish you'd never come in our life!" he or she is going to feel hurt. That's only normal too! And when people feel hurt, they sometimes act angry, and that isn't going to help the situation get any better. Instead, be respectful when you explain why you're upset. Be specific about what the problems are. If you are, you may find that the answers are easier to find than you might think.

And if none of this works, there are counselors who work especially with families in these situations, to help them find the answers they need. Don't be afraid to suggest this to your parents if you think it's what your family needs. Everyone needs some extra help coping with life sometimes, and that's what counselors are trained to do. In the same way you'd go to a doctor if you were sick, it's a good idea to go to a counselor when you need help finding new ways to solve problems or to deal with your feelings.

A New Family

It's takes a while to get comfortable with new people and new situations. But eventually, as time goes by, things get easier. You get to know each other. You learn things you enjoy about each other. You start to have fun together.

If you notice that's happening, at first you may feel as though you're being **disloyal** to your other home. But you don't need to feel that way. Both your parents want you to be happy. It will be easier for them to be happy with their new lives if they know you are happy too.

In the end, you may find you're lucky to have two sets of parents. Families get built in lots of different ways, but in the end, a family is a group of people who share a home—and who love and support each other. If you have MORE people who love you and are there for you if you need them, then you're pretty lucky!

Understand the Word

Disloyal means that you're not keeping your promises to someone or something, that you don't love someone or something as much as you once did, and that you have left someone or something behind in favor of someone or something else.

Questions to Think About

1. What do you think would be some of the hardest things about living in two homes?

2. Can you think of any good things about having two homes?

3. If you were Celeste, would you feel angry with your father for getting married again? Why or why not?

4. Do you think Celeste and Jordan will end up being friends? Why or why not?

5. How do you think Celeste and Whitney will get along with Marcy? What do you think will be the hardest thing for them as they get used to their new stepmother?

6. How do you think Jordan and Celeste's dad will get along? Why?

Further Reading

Blume, Judy. *It's Not the End of the World.* New York: Yearling, 1972.

Krementz, Jill. *How It Feels When Parents Divorce.* New York: Alfred A. Knopf, Inc., 1988.

Prokop, Michael S. *Divorce Happens to the Nicest Kids.* Warren, Ohio: Alegra House Publishers, 1996.

Find Out More on the Internet

A Kid's Guide to Divorce
http://kidshealth.org/kid/feeling/home_family/divorce.html

PBS Kids Go!
http://pbskids.org/itsmylife/family/divorce/index.html

The websites listed on this page were active at the time of publication. The publisher is not responsible for websites that have changed their address or discontinued operation since the date of publication. The publisher will review and update the websites upon each reprint.

Index

Picture Credits

Fotolia.com:
    Lisa F. Young: pg. 37
    Tatyana Gladskih: pg. 31

To the best knowledge of the publisher, all images not specifically credited are in the public domain. If any image has been inadvertently uncredited, please notify Harding House Publishing Service, 220 Front Street, Vestal, New York 13850, so that credit can be given in future printings.

About the Authors

Sheila Stewart has written several dozen books for young people, both fiction and nonfiction, although she especially enjoys writing fiction. She has a master's degree in English and now works as a writer and editor. She lives with her two children in a house overflowing with books, in the Southern Tier of New York State.

Rae Simons is a freelance author who has written numerous educational books for children and young adults. She also has degrees in psychology and special education, and she has worked with children encountering a range of troubles in their lives.

About the Consultant

Cindy Croft, M.A. Ed., is Director of the Center for Inclusive Child Care, a state-funded program with support from the McKnight Foundation, that creates, promotes, and supports pathways to successful inclusive care for all children. Its goal is inclusion and retention of children with disabilities and behavioral challenges in community child care settings. Cindy Croft is also on the faculty at Concordia University, where she teaches courses on young children with special needs and the emotional growth of young children. She is the author of several books, including *The Six Keys: Strategies for Promoting Children's Mental Health.*